Help the Environment

We Can Help the Environment

Rebecca Rissman

www.raintreepublishers.co.uk
Visit our website to find out
more information about
Raintree books.

To order:
☎ Phone 0845 6044371
🗎 Fax +44 (0) 1865 312263
🖥 Email myorders@capstonepub.co.uk

Customers from outside the UK please telephone +44 1865 312262

Raintree is an imprint of Capstone Global Library Limited,
a company incorporated in England and Wales having its
registered office at 7 Pilgrim Street, London, EC4V 6LB
– Registered company number: 6695582

Text © Capstone Global Library Limited 2009
First published in hardback in 2009
The moral rights of the proprietor have been asserted.

Edited by Rebecca Rissman, Siân Smith, and Charlotte Guillain
Designed by Kimberly Miracle and Joanna Malivoire
Picture research by Elizabeth Alexander

Printed in China by Leo Paper Group

ISBN 978 0 431194 19 6
13 12 11 10
10 9 8 7 6 5 4 3 2

British Library Cataloguing in Publication Data
Rissman, Rebecca
   We can help the environment. - (Acorn plus)
   1. Environmental protection - Citizen participation -
   Pictorial works - Juvenile literature
   I. Title
   363.7'0525

Acknowledgments

The author and publishers are grateful to the following for
permission to reproduce copyright material: Alamy pp. **7 left**,
21 (© Jim West), **11 left** (© Lourens Smak), **11 right** (© Ange),
13 right (© Stefan Kiefer / vario images), **16 left** (© Paul
Glendell), **18** (G Wolfgang Pölzer); © Capstone Global Library
Ltd pp. **9 left**, **9 right**, **22 middle** (Tudor Photography); Corbis
p.**8** (© LWA/Dann Tardif/Blend Images); Getty Images pp.**4**
(Taxi/ Eightfish), **6** (Stone/ Ben Osborne), **16 right** (Stone/
Victoria Snowber), **17 right** (Taxi /Gary Buss); iStockphoto
pp.**7 middle right** (© Ints Tomsons), **12 left** (© Hans F.
Meier), **12 right** (© Jon Schulte); NaturePL.com p.**19** (Aflo);
Photolibrary pp.**5** (Mark Henley/Imagestate), **10** (Dev Carr/
Cultura), **13 left** (Jeffrey Hamilton/ Stockbyte), **14** (Corbis),
15 (Creatas /Comstock), **20** (Momatiuk - Eastcott/ Flirt
Collection); Shutterstock **17 left** (© newphotoservice), **22 left**
(© Morgan Lane Photography), **22 right** (© newphotoservice),
7 middle left (© Morgan Lane Photography), **7 right** (© Feng
Yu).

Cover photograph of children picking up litter reproduced
with permission of Corbis/ © Leland Bobbé. Back cover
photograph reproduced with permission of Photolibrary (Dev
Carr/Cultura).

We would like to thank Nancy Harris and Adriana Scalise for
their help in the preparation of this book.

Every effort has been made to contact copyright holders of
any material reproduced in this book. Any omissions will
be rectified in subsequent printings if notice is given to the
publisher.

Contents

Some words are shown in bold, **like this**. They are explained in "Words to know" on page 23.

What is the environment?

The **environment** is the world around us.

People can hurt the environment in many ways.
We need to care for the environment.

Caring for the environment

There are many ways to care for the **environment**.

You can do something to help the environment every day.

Reusing

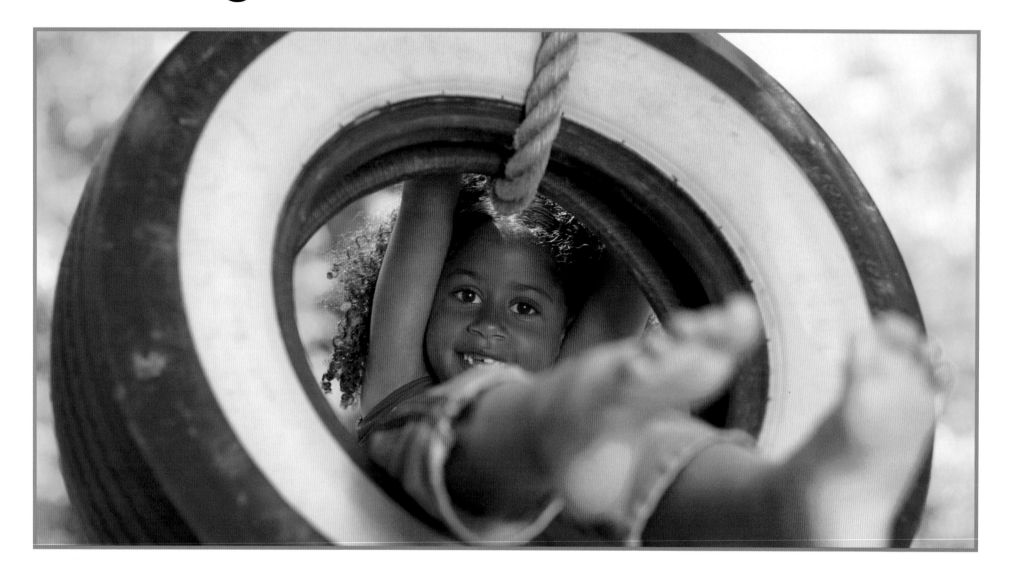

You can **reuse** old things instead of throwing them away. When you use an old tyre to make a swing you are reusing.

You can reuse old jars and boxes to keep things in.
When you reuse your things, you help the **environment**.

Recycling

You can **recycle**. Recycling turns old things into new things.

old paper

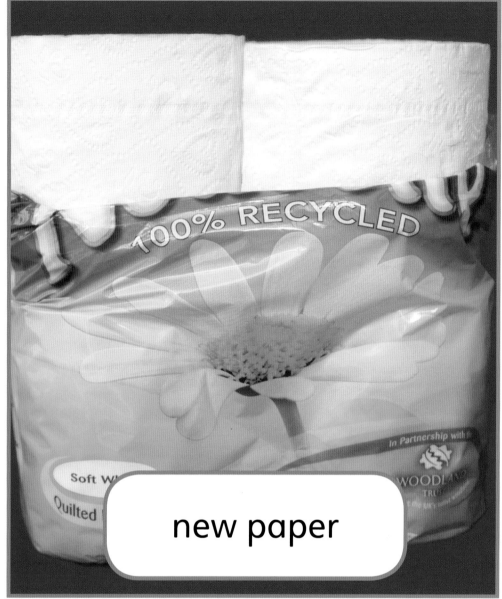

100% RECYCLED

Soft Wh

Quilted

WOODLA
TRU

new paper

You can recycle glass, metal, plastic, and paper.
When you recycle your things, you help the **environment**.

Saving energy

You can save **energy**. Energy makes many things work.

Lights use energy. When you turn off the lights, you save energy. Heating uses energy. Closing windows when the heating is on saves energy.

Cleaning up litter

You can clean up litter. Litter is rubbish that people leave on the ground. Litter is bad for the **environment**.

Never drop litter on the ground. When you clean up litter, you help the environment.

Saving water

You can save water. When you have a bath you use a lot of water. If you leave a tap running you use a lot of water.

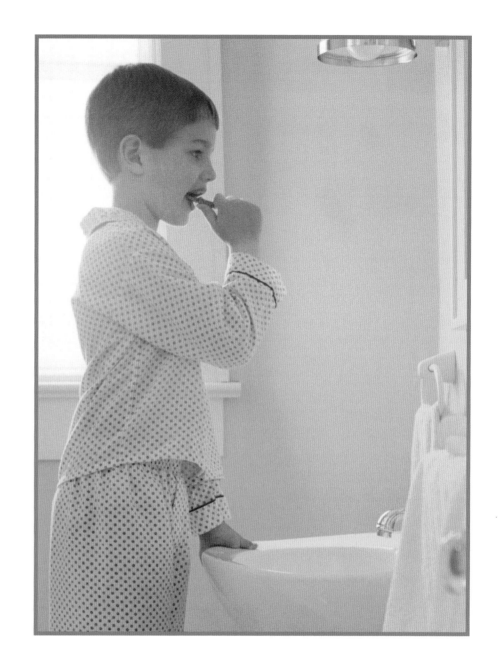

When you have a shower instead of a bath, you help the **environment**. When you turn off the tap while you brush your teeth, you help the environment.

Caring for nature

You can care for nature. You can care for plants.
You can care for animals.

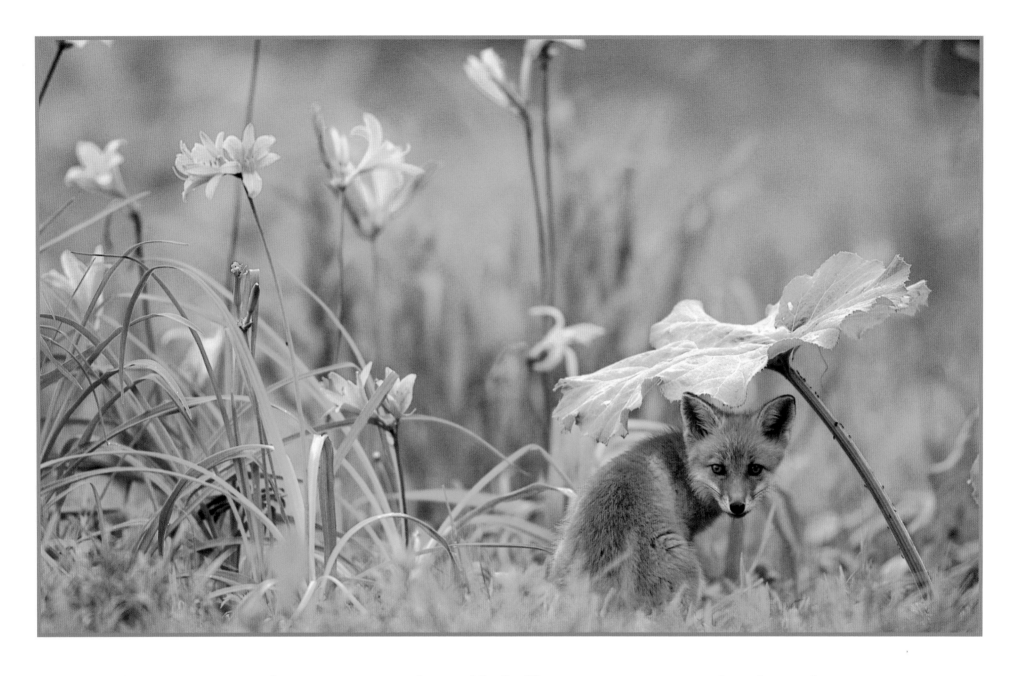

When you do not pick **wild flowers**, you help the **environment**. When you do not touch bird nests or **wild animals**, you help the environment.

Caring for the future

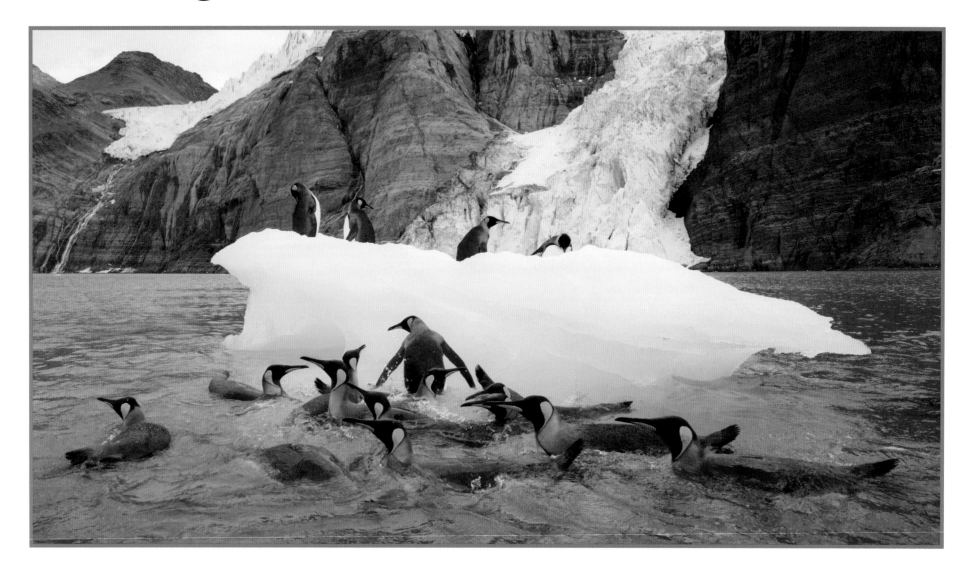

Caring for the **environment** will keep it clean and safe for the **future**.

We can care for the environment together.

How will you care for the environment today?

Words to know

energy
: the power to move, change, or grow. Things such as lights, computers, and cars need energy to make them work.

environment
: the world around us

future
: the time that is going to come or what is going to happen. The future can refer to a time minutes, days, or even years ahead.

pollution
: harmful dirt, waste gases or chemicals. The air, water, or land can be polluted.

reuse
: use again

recycle
: make old things into new things

wild animals
: animals that are not kept by people, for example animals that are not kept in zoos or as pets

wild flowers
: flowers that grow naturally and are not planted or grown by people

Index

Notes for parents and teachers

Before reading

Talk to the children about how the environment is the world around us. Plants and animals are part of our environment. When people drop litter they harm our environment. Ask children what they know about litter. What ways can we protect our environment? Together, begin creating a chart entitled "The environment."
Draw three columns and give them the following headings: "What you know", "What you want to know", and " What you've learned." Discuss the first two columns with the children and then fill in the first two columns together.

After reading

Continue discussing and filling in the chart with the children. Focus on the third column, "What you've learned." Ask children what they learned from this book. After children have listed their ideas, discuss how they can protect our environment by picking up litter, recycling, turning off a tap to save water, and only using lights when necessary. Help the children to create signs that show different ways to help the environment. If possible use recycled paper!